Ludwig van Beethoven

Symphony No. 1 in C major / C-Dur
Op. 21

Edited by / Herausgegeben von
Richard Clarke

T0081277

EULENBURG

EAS 192
ISBN 978-3-7957-6592-7
ISMN 979-0-2002-2624-9

© 2015 Ernst Eulenburg & Co GmbH, Mainz
for Europe excluding the British Isles
Ernst Eulenburg Ltd, London
for all other countries
CD ℗ 1996 NAXOS Rights US, Inc.
CD © 2015 Ernst Eulenburg Ltd, London

Ernst Eulenburg Ltd
48 Great Marlborough Street
London W1F 7BB

Contents / Inhalt

Preface

Dedicated to Baron Gottfried van Swieten
Composed: 1799/1800 in Vienna and its surroundings
First performance: 2 April 1800 at Vienna Hofburgtheater
Original publisher: Hoffmeister & Kühnel, Leipzig, 1801
Instrumentation: 2 Flutes, 2 Oboes, 2 Clarinets, 2 Bassoons –
2 Horns, 2 Trumpets – Timpani – Strings
Duration: ca. 25 minutes

It wasn't until 2 April 1880, when he was nearly 30 years old, that Beethoven ventured to put his First Symphony before the world, in a concert at the Vienna Burgtheater. It had been a long gestation. A first movement, slow movement and minuet were sketched out some time during 1795–6, but both the form and content of the finale seem to have eluded him. It wasn't until 1799 that he seems to have been struck by a bold new idea: the theme intended for the first movement was really more appropriate for the finale. The idea he subsequently conceived for the opening *Allegro con brio* is clearly much better suited to a movement in which development is crucial: it is relatively open-ended, and more easily broken down into characteristic motifs, each with its own potential for dramatic change. Still, the fact that what we now know as the finale's first subject was originally conceived for the Symphony's opening movement shows that Beethoven was already feeling the impulse to shift the weight of the argument towards the last movement – the revolutionary impulse that was to bear such remarkable fruit in the Third, Fifth and Ninth symphonies.

Despite the presence of undeniably forward-looking elements in the First Symphony, the work has had something of a bad press even from some staunch Beethoven champions. According to the Beethoven commentator, Lewis Lockwood, Beethoven 'played it safe rather than provoke his audience'.[1] For Denis Matthews, the First Symphony's 'moods are neutral, even conventional, as though Beethoven had decided to test his powers on safe ground before venturing into uncharted territory'.[2] It is true that the Symphony's formal layout is broadly that of a conventional Classical Era symphony, and that there are no innovations to match the highly dramatic integration of a slow introduction with a faster main movement in the *Pathétique* Sonata, Op.13 (1799). Yet for the anonymous critic of the first performance in the *Allgemeine Musikalische Zeitung* of Leipzig, the First Symphony showed 'considerable art, novelty and a wealth of

---

[1] Lewis Lockwood, *Beethoven: the Music and the Life* (New York, 2003), 148
[2] Denis Matthews, *Beethoven* (London, 1985), 152

ideas'.[3] Indeed the reviewer was somewhat put out by Beethoven's unusually prominent use of the wind instruments, 'so that the effect was more wind-band than full orchestral music'. That is indeed one novel feature of the First Symphony, but what also stands out is the imaginative interplay between winds and strings, at times approaching the kind of instrumental dialogue one finds in the finest chamber music of Haydn and Mozart.

Also noteworthy is the way Beethoven takes thematic integration to new lengths and levels of sophistication. The famously 'wrong' opening chord – apparently a dominant seventh of F major – arrestingly scored for pizzicato strings and sustained winds, is also the first note of a strikingly simple two-note motif, rising by a semitone. This is repeated, a fourth lower, in bar 2, extended in bars 3–4, then becomes the springboard of the hushed violin phrase that follows. Such close motivic working in a slow introduction is virtually unprecedented in a Classical Era symphony. But then the two-note rising semitone motif pervades the first theme of the *Allegro con brio*: in the repeated b–c' in the violins (bb13–16) and then the harmonically challenging wind chords that follow (bb17–19). Note also the masterly extended treatment of this motif in bb184–198, developing not only the semitonal motif but the sense of harmonic searching associated with it in the *Adagio molto* introduction. A rising semitone figure also haunts the quasi-fugal first theme of the *Andante cantabile con moto* (a'–b flat', bb2–3), while the Menuetto third movement seems positively obsessed with it, either rising, or falling, as in bars 9–10ff. The upward-surging scalic pattern of the Menuetto's first theme then becomes the basis of the witty transitional *Adagio* introduction to the finale, in which the initial rising figure grows by steps, then races into action as the opening phrase of the finale's first theme.

By common consent it is the Menuetto (a fiery Beethovenian Scherzo in all but name) that stands out in the First Symphony. Lockwood concedes that it is a 'brilliant, ambitious' achievement, 'with a far-reaching modulatory scheme in its second section'. But is Lockwood right to claim that its 'fullness of realization [...] eludes the other movements'?[4] Examination of the ingenious and imaginative motivic working would suggest otherwise. As to the work's spirit, perhaps the best comment on that was made by Tovey. For him, the First Symphony is: 'a fitting farewell to the 18th century. It has more of the true 19th-century Beethoven in its depths than he allows to appear on the surface. Its style is that of the Comedy of Manners, as translated by Mozart into the music of his opera and of his most light-hearted works of symphonic and chamber music. The fact that it is comedy from beginning to end is prophetic of changes in music no less profound than those which the French Revolution brought about in social organism.'[5]

Nowhere is that clearer than in the comically tentative *Adagio* that introduces the finale, the theme like a butterfly wriggling free of its chrysalis then bursting into free flight.

Stephen Johnson

---

[3] *Allgemeine musikalische Zeitung* 3 (1800/1801), No.3 of 15 October 1800, col.49; quoted from Elliot Forbes (ed.), *Thayer's Life of Beethoven* (New York, 1967), 255

[4] Lockwood, op. cit., 148

[5] Donald Francis Tovey, *Essays in Musical Analysis*, Vol.1 (London, 1935), 21

Vorwort

dem Freiherrn Gottfried van Swieten gewidmet
komponiert: 1799/1800 in Wien und Umgebung
Uraufführung: 2. April 1800 im Wiener Hofburgtheater
Originalverlag: Hoffmeister & Kühnel, Leipzig, 1801
Orchesterbesetzung: 2 Flöten, 2 Oboen, 2 Klarinetten, 2 Fagotte –
2 Hörner, 2 Trompeten – Pauken – Streicher
Spieldauer: etwa 25 Minuten

Beethoven war fast 30 Jahre alt, als er es wagte, der Welt seine erste Sinfonie bei einem Konzert am 2. April 1880 im Wiener Burgtheater zu präsentieren. Das Werk hatte eine lange Entstehungszeit. Einen ersten Satz, einen langsamen Satz und ein Menuett skizzierte er bereits zwischen 1795 und 1796, aber sowohl formal als auch inhaltlich wollte ihm für das Finale keine passende Lösung einfallen. Erst 1799 hatte er einen mutigen neuen Einfall, nämlich dass sich das ursprünglich für den ersten Satz vorgesehene Thema viel besser für das Finale eignete. Die Idee, die er dann für das eröffnende Allegro con brio entworfen hat, passt deutlich besser zu einem Satz, in dem die Durchführung entscheidend ist: Sie ist relativ offen und in charakteristische Motive aufgegliedert, welche jeweils eigenes Potenzial für einen dramatischen Wechsel bergen. Dennoch zeigt die Tatsache, dass das, was wir heute als erstes Thema des Finales kennen ursprünglich für den Eröffnungssatz der Sinfonie gedacht war, dass Beethoven schon damals den Impuls verspürte, den thematischen Schwerpunkt in den letzten Satz zu verlagern. Dieser revolutionäre Impuls sollte später eine besondere Bedeutung in der dritten, fünften und neunten Sinfonie bekommen.

Obwohl es in der 1. Sinfonie unbestritten zukunftsweisende Elemente gibt, hatte das Werk schlechte Kritiken bekommen, sogar von einigen treuen Beethoven-Verfechtern. Laut dem Beethoven-Spezialisten Lewis Lockwood „[…] schlug sich Beethoven lieber auf die sichere Seite, anstatt zu provozieren […]."[1] Für Denis Matthews sind in der 1. Sinfonie die „Stimmungen neutral, nahezu konventionell, als ob Beethoven beschlossen hätte, seine Kräfte auf sicherem Boden zu testen, bevor er sich auf Neuland wagte."[2] Es stimmt, dass der formale Aufbau der Sinfonie einer traditionellen klassischen Sinfonie folgt und dass es keine Neuerungen gibt, die sich mit der höchst dramatischen Kombination einer langsamen Einleitung mit dem schnelleren Hauptsatz wie in der *Pathétique*-Sonate, op. 13 (1799), vergleichen lassen. Für den anonymen

---

[1] Lewis Lockwood: *Beethoven. Seine Musik. Sein Leben*, Kassel 2009, S. 115.
[2] Denis Matthews: *Beethoven*, London 1985, S. 152.

Kritiker der *Allgemeinen musikalischen Zeitung* aus Leipzig zeigte die 1. Sinfonie bei der Erst-
aufführung dennoch „sehr viel Kunst, Neuheit und Reichtum an Ideen."[3] Allerdings war der
Kritiker über Beethovens ungewöhnlich auffällige Verwendung der Blasinstrumente etwas
verärgert und schrieb: „Nur waren die Blasinstrumente gar zu viel angewendet, so daß sie
mehr Harmonie als ganze Orchestermusik war". Dies ist in der Tat ein neues Merkmal der
1. Sinfonie. Was aber auch auffällt, ist das fantasievolle Wechselspiel zwischen den Bläsern
und Streichern, das zuweilen an die Art der instrumentalen Dialoge erinnert, die man in
Haydns und Mozarts bester Kammermusik finden kann.

Beachtenswert ist auch die Art, wie Beethoven die thematische Einbindung mit Raffinesse zu
neuen Längen führt. Der berühmte „falsche" Eröffnungsakkord – scheinbar ein Dominant-
septakkord in F-Dur –, der interessanterweise mit Streichern im Pizzicato und ausgehaltenen
Bläsern besetzt ist, bildet zugleich den ersten Ton eines erstaunlich einfachen Motivs. Dieses
besteht aus nur zwei Noten, die in einem Halbtonschritt aufsteigen. Es wird in Takt 2 eine
Quarte tiefer wiederholt, in den Takten 3 und 4 dient es dann als Sprungbrett für die folgende
Phrase der gedämpften Violinen. Solch eine dichte motivische Arbeit in einer langsamen Einleitung gab es in einer klassischen Sinfonie bisher noch nicht. Aber schließlich durchdringt
das aufsteigende Halbton-Motiv das erste Thema des Allegro con brio: in den wiederholt auf-
tretenden Tönen h-c' in den Violinen (T. 13–16) und dann in den folgenden harmonisch
anspruchsvollen Akkorden der Bläser (T. 17–19). Zu beachten ist auch die meisterhaft aus-
gedehnte Verarbeitung dieses Motivs in den Takten 184–198, wobei nicht nur das Halbton-
Motiv weiterentwickelt wird, sondern auch die damit verbundene Absicht einer harmonischen
Suche in der Einleitung des Adagio molto. Eine aufsteigende Halbtonfigur zieht sich auch durch
das quasi-fugierte erste Thema des Andante cantabile con moto (a'-b', T. 2–3). Im dritten
Menuett-Satz findet sich diese Figur immer wieder, entweder aufsteigend oder absteigend
wie in den Takten 9–10ff. Das aufwärtssteigende Tonleitermodell aus dem ersten Thema des
Menuetts bildet schließlich die Grundlage für die geistreiche vorläufige Adagio-Einleitung
des Finales, in dem die anfänglich aufsteigende Figur stufenweise wächst und schließlich in
die Eröffnungsphrase des ersten Themas des Finales mündet.

Nach allgemeiner Auffassung sticht das Menuett (ein im wahrsten Sinne des Wortes glühendes
beethovensches Scherzo) aus der 1. Sinfonie hervor. Lockwood gibt zu, dass es „ein langer,
brillanter, ambitionierter Satz mit ausgreifenden Modulationen im zweiten Abschnitt und
einer Stringenz, die diejenige der anderen Sätze weit übersteigt"[4], ist. Eine Untersuchung des
raffinierten und einfallsreichen motivischen Materials würde auf etwas anderes hindeuten. Was
den Geist des Werkes betrifft, so schrieb vielleicht Tovey die beste Interpretation. Für ihn ist
die 1. Sinfonie „ein passender Abschied vom 18. Jahrhundert. Im tiefsten Innern hat sie mehr
von dem wahren Beethoven des 19. Jahrhunderts in sich als er es oberflächlich zu erscheinen
erlaubt. Sie ist im Stile einer „Comedy of Manners" [deutsch: Sittenstück] komponiert, wie sie
von Mozart in seinen Opern und seinen heitersten sinfonischen sowie kammermusikalischen
Werken umgesetzt wurde. Die Tatsache, dass es sich vom Anfang bis zum Schluss um eine

---

[3] *Allgemeine musikalische Zeitung* 3 (1800/1801), Nr. 3 vom 15. Oktober 1800, Sp. 49.
[4] Lewis Lockwood: *Beethoven. Seine Musik. Sein Leben*, Kassel 2009, S. 114.

Komödie handelt, kündigt Veränderungen in der Musik an, die nicht weniger tiefgreifend sind als jene, die die französische Revolution im gesellschaftlichen Bereich mit sich gebracht hat."[5]

Nirgendwo sonst wird dies deutlicher als in dem komisch zaghaften Adagio, welches das Finale einleitet; das Thema ist wie ein Schmetterling, der sich von seinem Kokon befreit und sich dann in den Gleitflug stürzt.

Stephen Johnson
Übersetzung: Uta Pastowski

[5] Donald Francis Tovey: *Essays in Musical Analysis*, Bd. 1, London 1935, S. 21.

Symphony No. 1

À son Excellence Monsieur le Baron van Swieten

Ludwig van Beethoven
(1770–1827)
Op. 21

I. Adagio molto (♪ = 88)

EAS 192

Edited by Richard Clarke
© 2015 Ernst Eulenburg Ltd, London
and Ernst Eulenburg & Co GmbH, Mainz

Allegro con brio ($\downarrow$ = 112)

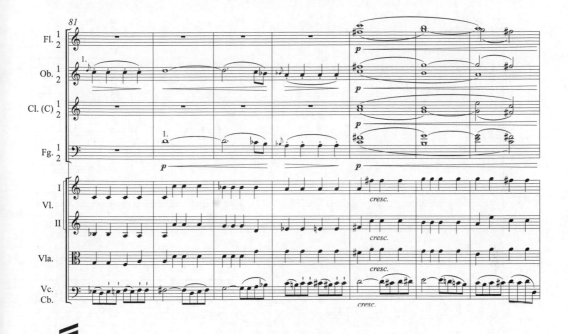

C
174
181
Fl. 1 2
Ob. 1 2
Cl. (C) 1 2
Fg. 1 2
Cor. (C) 1 2
Tr. (C) 1 2
Timp.
I
Vl.
II
Vla.
Vc.
Cb.
a 2
1.

22

II. Andante cantabile con moto (♪ = 120)

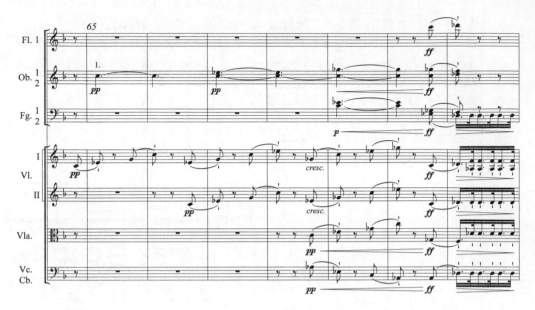

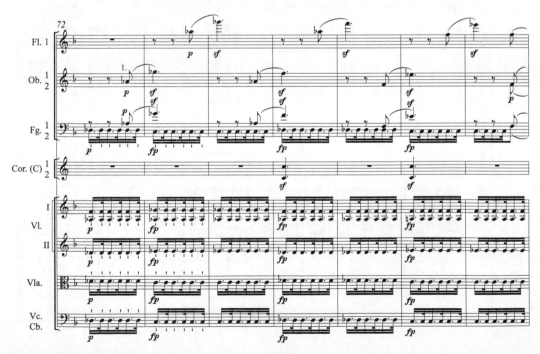

27

EAS 192

III. Menuetto

Allegro molto e vivace (♩. = 108)

Trio

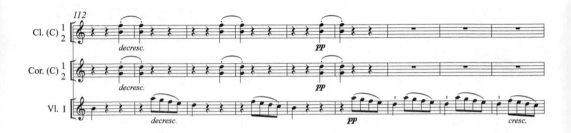

IV. Finale

Printed in China

THE ART OF SCORE-READING

The first steps

A score contains the entire musical text of a musical work in order that the conductor and everyone who wants to study the piece more thoroughly can see exactly which passages are being played by the orchestra or ensemble. The parts of the individual instruments are arranged in such a way that all notes played at the same time are written one below the other.

Scores help to listen to, understand and interpret musical works. Those who only listen to music are unaware of many important details which, after some practice, become apparent when reading the score while listening to the music. The clear structure of the score helps to easily understand the compositional style and the characteristic features of a piece – this is a prerequisite not only for any analysis but also for the musician's own performance and interpretation.

The simplest method of score-reading is to read an individual part by concentrating on an individual part that can be heard particularly well. The most suitable pieces to begin with are concertos with solo instruments such as Beethoven's Romance in F major for violin and orchestra (example 1) or orchestral songs (with them, one may easily follow the text). Furthermore, in many classical orchestral works, it is quite easy to follow the lead part of the principal violin, or the bass part in baroque compositions for orchestra.

The next step is to try to change from one part to another and vice versa and follow the part that is leading. Little by little, you learn to find distinctive parts you hear in the score as well and follow them in the corresponding staff. This can be very easily tried out with Beethoven's Symphony No. 5 (example 2). To read the score, it is also helpful to count the bars. This technique is rather useful in the case of confusing or complex scores, such as those of contemporary music, and is particularly suitable when you do not want to lag behind in any case. It should be your aim, however, to eventually give up counting the bars and to read the score by first following individual parts and then going over to section-by-section or selective reading (see next page).

Example 1 · from: Romance for violin and orchestra in F major by Beethoven

Example 2 · from: Symphony No. 5 C-minor by Beethoven

Further score-reading techniques

Example 3 · from: Symphony No. 100 G major 'Military' by Haydn

Example 4 · from: Symphony No. 41 C major 'Jupiter' by W. A. Mozart

Section-by-section reading

This technique is suitable for application in the 'Military' Symphony by Haydn (example 3). In bb. 260-264, the parts are mostly in parallel motion so that it is quite easy to take in the section as a whole. In the strings, the texture is homophonic (i.e. all instruments play the same rhythm), consisting of tone repetitions in the lower parts while there is a little more movement in the part of the first violin. At the same time, the tones of the winds are stationary (i.e. long sustained notes), serving as harmonic filling-in. If need be, they can also be read en bloc.

Such block-like structures often consist of unison figures (= all instruments play the same), such as at the beginning of Mozart's Jupiter Symphony (example 4). Here, the score-reading can first be limited to the strings section which carries the melody alone in bb. 3-4 and contains all important information.

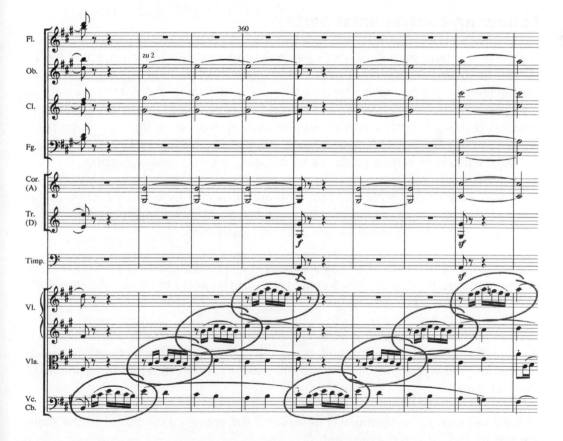

Example 5 · from: Symphony No. 7 A major by Beethoven

Selective reading

Using this technique, you concentrate on selected parts (lead parts, conspicuous passages) in the score. In the excerpt from Beethoven's Symphony No. 7 (example 5), it is the semiquaver motif that, originating with the violoncellos and basses and pervading the string parts twice, is particularly well suited. The stationary tones of the winds, consisting only of the note E in various octave positions in bb. 358-363, form the harmonic foundation and play a subordinate role in score-reading. Though they are briefly noticed, it is the strings and especially the conspicuous semiquaver motif pervading the individual parts that are to be followed.

With both score-reading techniques which should be chosen according to the nature of the passage in question, it is not important in the beginning to be able to follow at once all tones and harmonies. What matters more is to recognize and comprehend sequences of movement. Everything else comes with experience.

Following contrapuntal parts

The present excerpt from Brahms's Requiem (example 6) is polyphonic, i.e. one has to be able to follow several equal parts either alternately (without lagging behind) or simultaneously. But by looking for parallel parts in the score, the notation which, at first glance, seems to be overcrowded soon becomes clearer. For example, Brahms allocates orchestral parts to each choral part. As a consequence, there are many parts written in the score but considerably fewer independent parts actually played. Hence, the large amount of written music can be reduced to a manageable quantity.

The flute, clarinet, first violins and soprano are in parallel motion. Furthermore, the tenor of oboe and viola is supported by a much-expanded, yet parallel part. The violoncellos and bassoons too are in almost parallel motion.

The low winds and strings as well as the timpani played simultaneously with the polyphonic parts are fill-in parts which consist only of stationary tones (sustained notes). They do not need to be followed upon first reading of the score.

Seen as a whole, this excerpt is most suitable for focussing on the soprano voice as it is coupled with two instruments and, being the highest voice, can be heard very well. In addition, the text is an aid to orientation, making it easier to return from brief trips to other parts.

In fugal sections, score-reading will be easier if the entries of the theme in the score are first looked for and then marked.

Example 6 · from: A German Requiem by Brahms

The score at a glance

A **Bar lines** are solid vertical lines within the instrument sections.

B The **bar numbers** are an aid to orientation in the score. Sometimes capital letters, so-called rehearsal letters, are used instead of numbers.

C The system of parallel lines on and between which the notes are written is called **staff** (or stave). The instrument abbreviation in front of each line (here, Fl. is for 'flute') indicates to which instrument(s) the line(s) refer(s).

D The **barline at the left-hand end** of the staves connects all staves to form the **system**.

E In addition to the barline at the left-hand end of the staves, **angular brackets** connect the individual groups of instruments in a score (wind, brass and string instruments). Within these groups, the instruments are arranged according to their pitch, with the highest-pitched instrument mentioned first.
Today, the common order of instrumental parts in the score is as follows, from top to bottom:
· wind instruments
· brass instruments
· percussion instruments
· harp, piano, celesta
· solo instrument(s)
· solo voices
· choir
· string instruments

F When there are two systems on a page, they are separated from each other by two parallel **diagonal strokes**.

G Instruments the names of which are followed by 'in Bb' or (Bb) are **transposing instruments**. In this case, (Bb) indicates that the notated C is played as Bb, i.e. all tones are played a tone lower than notated. Most of the transposing instruments are easily recognizable in the score thanks to these additions. However, there are also transposing instruments without such indications in the score, such as:
· piccolo flute (in C / an octave higher)
· cor anglais (in F / a fifth lower)
· contrabassoon (in C / an octave lower)
· double bass (in C / an octave lower)

H The transposing brass instruments have no general signature but, if need be, accidentals preceding the respective tone.

I The viola part is notated in the **alto clef**, the parts of violoncello and bassoon sometimes in the **tenor clef**. Both clefs are easy to read when the player realizes that the clef frames the note C1:
alto clef   tenor clef   treble clef

J Any change of key or time is marked by a **double bar**. The alla-breve sign following in this example (¢), like the sign for four-four time (c), is a relic from an old notational practice and stands for two-two time.

Section-by-section reading:
For parts which, rhythmically, move in parallel motion.

Selective reading:
The lead part is followed.

from: Symphony No. 4 Bb by Beethoven

A **Tempo indications** (sometimes in connection with metronome markings) are used by the composer to indicate how fast a piece shall be played.

B In the winds, two parts are usually brought together in one line. If they play the same note, the note head either has two stems or 'a2' written above it.

C Two-part chords in the staves of the strings are played by one player. If the parts shall be divided, **divisi** (divided) is written in the score. Then, at each desk, one player plays the upper notes and another player the lower notes.

D When an instrumental part contains a long rest, as in this flute part for example, its staff is often omitted until the next entry of the instrument, thus saving space. In addition, there are less page-turns, and the playing parts are arranged much clearer.

E In order to save space and arrange phrases or groups of notes more clearly, so-called abbreviations are used occasionally. The sign 𝅗𝅥 stands for ♩♩♩♩, with the minim indicating the duration of the repetitions and the stroke crossing the stem indicating the value of the notes to be repeated (1 stroke = quaver, 2 strokes = semiquaver, etc.). Cf. also the viola in b. 43 in which the repeated notes are first written out and then abbreviated.

Score-Reading with pupils and students!

Mozart for the classroom

For further information, see at: www.eulenburg.de

Eulenburg

1507 02 MA 06/06

DIE KUNST
DES PARTITURLESENS

Der erste Einstieg

Eine Partitur enthält den gesamten Notentext eines Musikwerkes, damit der Dirigent und jeder, der sich näher mit dem Stück beschäftigen will, genau nachvollziehen kann, was das Orchester oder das Ensemble spielt. Dabei sind die Instrumente so angeordnet, dass alle Noten, die zur gleichen Zeit erklingen, genau untereinander stehen. Partituren helfen beim Hören, Begreifen und Interpretieren von Musikliteratur. Wer nur zuhört, erkennt viele kostbare Kleinigkeiten nicht, die beim Mitlesen nach ein wenig Übung regelrecht sichtbar werden. Der Kompositionsstil und die Charakteristik eines Werkes lassen sich mit der übersichtlichen Partitur schnell begreifen – das ist nicht nur Grundvoraussetzung für jede Analyse, sondern auch für das eigene Spiel.

Die einfachste Methode beim Partiturlesen ist das Verfolgen einer Einzelstimme. Bei diesem Verfahren konzentriert man sich auf eine einzelne Stimme, die besonders gut zu hören ist. Zum Einstieg eignen sich dabei besonders gut Konzerte mit Soloinstrumenten wie die Romanze in F-Dur für Violine und Orchester von Beethoven (Beispiel 1) oder Orchesterlieder (bei letzteren kann man sich leicht am Text orientieren). Weiterhin kann man bei vielen klassischen Orchesterwerken die führende Stimme der ersten Violine gut verfolgen, sowie bei barocken Kompositionen für Orchester die Bass-Stimme.

In einem nächsten Schritt kann man versuchen, zwischen den Stimmen zu wechseln und jeweils die Stimme zu verfolgen, die gerade führend ist. Nach und nach lernt man dabei markante Stimmen, die man hört, auch in der Partitur zu finden und im entsprechenden Notensystem zu verfolgen. Besonders anschaulich kann man das mittels Beethovens 5. Symphonie erproben (Beispiel 2). Eine weitere Hilfe beim Lesen der Partitur kann auch das Mitzählen der Takte sein. Dieses Verfahren hilft bei unübersichtlichen oder komplexen Partituren wie etwa zeitgenössischer Musik und eignet sich besonders, wenn man den Anschluss auf keinen Fall verlieren möchte. Ziel sollte es jedoch sein, das Mitzählen der Takte gänzlich zu verlassen und die Partitur zunächst anhand einzelner Stimmen und dann im Wechsel von blockweisem bzw. selektivem Lesen zu verfolgen (siehe nächste Seite).

Beispiel 1 · aus: Romanze für Violine und Orchester F-Dur von Beethoven

Beispiel 2 · aus: Symphonie Nr. 5 c-moll von Beethoven

Weitere Methoden des Partiturlesens

Beispiel 3 · aus: Symphonie Nr. 100 G-Dur „Militär" von Haydn

Beispiel 4 · aus: Symphonie Nr. 41 C-Dur „Jupiter" von W. A. Mozart

Blockweises Lesen

Diese Methode bietet sich in der Militär-Symphonie von Haydn an (Beispiel 3). In den T. 260-264 sind die Stimmen weitgehend parallel geführt, so dass man sie gut im Ganzen überblicken kann. In den Streichern haben wir einen homophonen Satz (d.h. alle Stimmen spielen den gleichen Rhythmus), der in den unteren Stimmen aus Tonwiederholungen besteht, während die erste Violine etwas bewegter ist. Gleichzeitig erklingen in den Bläserstimmen Liegetöne (d.h. lang ausgehaltene Töne), die als harmonischer Füllstoff dienen. Sie können bei Bedarf auch im Block gelesen werden.

Oft bestehen solche blockhaften Gebilde auch aus unisono-Figuren (= alle Stimmen spielen dasselbe), wie z.B. am Beginn der Jupiter-Symphonie von Mozart (Beispiel 4). Hier kann man sich beim Lesen zunächst nur auf den Streicherblock beschränken, der in den T. 3-4 alleine die Melodie weiterführt und bereits alle wichtigen Informationen enthält.

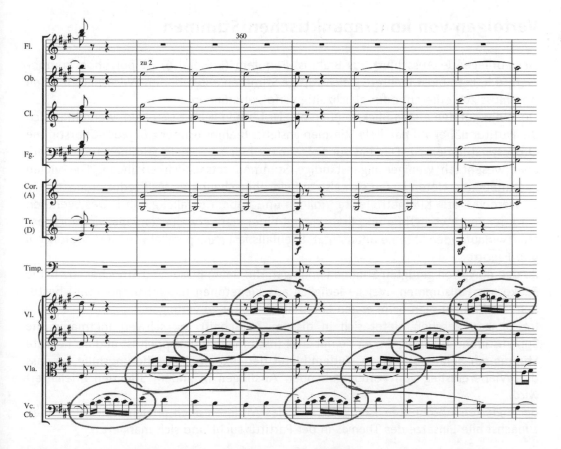

Beispiel 5 · aus: Symphonie Nr. 7 A-Dur von Beethoven

Selektives Lesen

Bei dieser Methode orientiert man sich anhand ausgewählter Stimmen (führende Stimmen, auffällige Stellen) in der Partitur. Im Ausschnitt aus Beethovens 7. Symphonie (Beispiel 5) ist hierzu das Sechzehntelmotiv geeignet, das zweimal von den Celli und Bässen ausgehend durch die Streicherstimmen wandert. Die Liegetöne der Bläser, die in den T. 358-363 sogar nur aus dem Ton e in unterschiedlichen Oktavlagen bestehen, bilden die harmonische Grundierung und spielen beim Lesen der Partitur eine untergeordnete Rolle. Man nimmt sie kurz wahr, verfolgt jedoch die Streicher und dort insbesondere das auffällige Sechzehntelmotiv in seiner Wanderung durch die einzelnen Stimmen.

Bei beiden Leseformen, zwischen denen man übrigens je nach Beschaffenheit der Stelle wechseln sollte, kommt es am Anfang nicht darauf an, sofort alle Töne und Harmonien verfolgen zu können. Viel wichtiger ist es, Bewegungsabläufe zu erkennen und nachzuvollziehen. Alles Weitere kommt mit der Erfahrung.

Verfolgen von kontrapunktischen Stimmen

Der vorliegende Ausschnitt aus Brahms' Requiem (Beispiel 6) ist polyphon komponiert, d.h. man muss mehrere gleichwertige Stimmen entweder im Wechsel (ohne den Anschluss zu verlieren) oder gleichzeitig verfolgen können.

Doch das auf den ersten Blick so übervolle Notenbild lichtet sich bald, wenn man sich die Partitur näher auf parallele Stimmen ansieht. Brahms ordnet z.B. jeder Chorstimme Orchesterstimmen zu. Das hat zur Folge, dass hier zwar viele Stimmen notiert sind, aber wesentlich weniger eigenständige Stimmen tatsächlich erklingen. Die vielen geschriebenen Noten lassen sich also auf ein überschaubares Maß reduzieren.

So werden Flöte, Klarinette, erste Violinen und Sopran parallel geführt. Des Weiteren wird der Tenor von Oboe und Bratsche mit einer stark erweiterten, aber dennoch parallel verlaufenden Stimme unterstützt. Ebenfalls fast ganz parallel verlaufen Violoncelli und Fagotte.

Zu den polyphon gefügten Stimmen erklingen die tiefen Bläser und Streicher sowie die Pauke mit Füllstimmen, welche lediglich aus Liegetönen (ausgehaltene Töne) bestehen. Sie braucht man beim ersten Lesen nicht weiter zu verfolgen.

Im Ganzen gesehen bietet sich in diesem Ausschnitt an, schwerpunktmäßig die Sopranstimme zu verfolgen, da sie mit zwei Instrumenten gekoppelt ist und als höchste Stimme gut herauszuhören ist. Zudem bietet der Text eine Orientierungshilfe, so dass der Wiedereinstieg von vorübergehenden Ausflügen in andere Stimmen erleichtert wird.

Bei fugierten Abschnitten kann man sich das Mitlesen auch erleichtern, indem man zunächst alle Einsätze des Themas in der Partitur sucht und sich markiert.

Beispiel 6 · aus: Ein deutsches Requiem von Brahms

Die Partitur im Überblick

A **Taktstriche** sind innerhalb der Instrumentengruppen durchgezogen.

B Die **Taktzahlen** erleichtern die Orientierung in der Partitur. Manchmal dienen hierzu auch Großbuchstaben, sog. Studierbuchstaben.

C Eine einzelne Zeile der Partitur nennt man **Notensystem**. Für welche(s) Instrument(e) sie steht, zeigt der **Instrumentenvorsatz** an (hier Fl. für Flöte).

D Der **Kopfstrich** verbindet alle Notensysteme miteinander zu einer **Akkolade**.

E Zusätzlich zum Kopfstrich fassen **gerade Klammern** die einzelnen Instrumentengruppen (Holz-, Blech- und Streichinstrumente) zusammen. Innerhalb dieser Gruppen sind die Instrumente nach Tonlage geordnet, wobei das höchste an oberster Stelle steht.
Die heute übliche Partituranordnung lautet von oben nach unten:
· Holzblasinstrumente
· Blechblasinstrumente
· Schlaginstrumente
· Harfe, Klavier, Celesta
· Soloinstrument(e)
· Solostimmen
· Chor
· Streichinstrumente

F Stehen zwei Akkoladen auf einer Seite, werden sie durch zwei **Schrägstriche** voneinander abgetrennt.

G Steht hinter dem Instrumentennamen z.B. „in B" oder (B), handelt es sich um ein **transponierendes Instrument**. In diesem Fall deutet das (B) an, dass das notierte C als B erklingt, also alle Noten einen Ton tiefer erklingen als sie notiert sind. Die meisten transponierenden Instrumente sind in der Partitur durch diese Zusätze leicht zu erkennen. Es gibt aber auch transponierende Instrumente ohne eine entsprechende Angabe in der Partitur, wie z.B.:
Piccoloflöte (in c/eine Oktave höher)
Englischhorn (in f/eine Quinte tiefer)
Kontrafagott (in c/eine Oktave tiefer)
Kontrabass (in c/eine Oktave tiefer)

H Die transponierenden Blechblasinstrumente haben keine Generalvorzeichen, sondern bei Bedarf Versetzungszeichen, die direkt vor der jeweiligen Note stehen.

I Die Viola oder Bratsche wird im **Alt- bzw. Bratschenschlüssel** notiert, die Stimmen des Violoncellos und Fagotts manchmal im **Tenorschlüssel**. Beide Schlüssel sind leicht zu lesen, wenn man sich klarmacht, dass der Schlüssel den Ton c1 umrahmt, also:

Alt-   Tenor-   Violinschlüssel

J Vor einem Wechsel der Ton- oder Taktart steht immer ein **Doppelstrich**. Das hier folgende Alla-Breve-Zeichen (¢) ist ebenso wie das Zeichen für den 4/4-Takt (c) ein Relikt aus einer älteren Notationspraxis und steht für den 2/2-Takt.

Blockweises Lesen:
Bei rhythmisch parallelgeführten Stimmen.

A

B

C

D

Selektives Lesen: Man verfolgt die führende Stimme.

E

aus: Symphonie Nr. 4 B-Dur von Beethoven

A Durch die **Tempoangabe** (manchmal mit einer Metronomzahl verbunden) gibt der Komponist an, wie schnell ein Stück gespielt werden soll.

B Bei den Bläsern werden in der Regel zwei Stimmen in einer Notenzeile zusammengefasst. Spielen sie den gleichen Ton, erhält der Notenkopf zwei Hälse oder es steht a2 darüber.

C Zweistimmige Akkorde in den Notensystemen der Streicher werden von einem Spieler gespielt. Will man die Stimmen aufteilen, schreibt man **divisi** (geteilt). Dann spielt an jedem Pult ein Spieler die oberen und ein Spieler die unteren Noten.

D Hat eine Stimme, wie hier die Flöte, längere Zeit Pause, wird ihr Notensystem oft bis zum erneuten Einsatz der Stimme weggelassen. So wird Platz gespart, man muß weniger blättern und die erklingenden Stimmen sind übersichtlicher angeordnet.

E Um Platz zu sparen und Tonfolgen übersichtlicher zu gestalten, verwendet man gelegentlich sogenannte **Abbreviaturen (Faulenzer)**. Das hier verwendete Zeichen ♩ steht für ♪♪♪♪, wobei die Halbe Note die Dauer der Wiederholungen anzeigt und der Strich durch den Notenhals den Wert der zu wiederholenden Noten (1 Strich = Achtel, 2 = Sechzehntel usw.). Vgl. auch die Viola in T. 43, in der zunächst die Repetitionen ausgeschrieben und dann abgekürzt sind.

Partiturlesen im Klassensatz

Diese kurze Einführung können Sie als kostenloses Faltblatt bestellen – gern auch im Klassensatz!

Faltblatt "Die Kunst des Partiturlesens"
Bestellnummer: ETP 9999-99 (kostenlos)

Die passende Ergänzung für Klassen- und Unterrichtsräume:

Plakat A2 "Die Partitur im Überblick"
Bestellnummer ETP 9950-99 (kostenlos)

Mozart im Klassensatz

Ein Lebens- und Reisebild

Mozart war nicht nur einer der größten Komponisten, sondern auch einer der besten Pianisten des 18. Jahrhunderts. Wie heutige Virtuosen verbrachte er große Teile seines Lebens auf Konzertreisen zwischen den führenden Höfen und großen Städten seiner Zeit. Diese kleine Broschüre entfaltet ein Panorama des europäischen Musiklebens, das den Hintergrund für Mozarts Schaffen bildete. Eine Kurzbiographie und ein kleiner Einblick in seine Schreibweise runden das Bild ab.

Faltblatt "Mozart. Ein Lebens- und Reisebild"
Bestellnummer ETP 9990-99 (kostenlos)

Weitere Informationen unter www.eulenburg.de

Eulenburg